urgent!

igniting a passion
for Jesus

Joe Donahue

ISBN 978-0-9826561-1-2

Printed in the United States of America by
Lightning Source, Inc.

Text Design by Debbie Patrick, visionrun.com

Unless otherwise indicated, all Scripture quotations are taken from the Holy Bible, New Living Translation, copyright © 1996, 2004, 2007 by Tyndale House Foundation. Used by permission of Tyndale House Publishers, Inc., Carol Stream, Illinois 60188. All rights reserved.

Free Church Press
P.O. Box 1075
Carrollton, GA 30112

Foreword

Some 400 years after Christ, a most remarkable book was published. In a scandal of almost biblical proportions, Christianity's most erudite theologian bared his soul for the world to see.

The bishop in the prominent city of Hippo (present day Annaba, Algeria), Augustine (AD 354-430) had already established himself as a wise leader, engaging teacher and prominent theologian. Over the course of his seventy-five years on the earth, Augustine would shape Patristic Christianity, writing such seminal works as *City of God*, *On the Trinity* and *On Christian Doctrine*. His writings would guide Christian thought and be regarded as the strongest voice of Christian philosophy for almost a thousand years, until Aquinas in the Middle Ages.

Yet at the rough age of forty, Augustine made a decision that would forever change Christian writing. He penned the first major Christian autobiography, entitled *Confessions*. Few Christians had ever dared to open their lives up to such scrutiny. With transparent vulnerability, Augustine wrote of his sinful past, sexual addictions and shameful decisions. He exposed his inner turmoil for all to see. He wrote of his search for truth through cults and false philosophies. He wrote of the heartache of his godly mother.

Very few works exist like it, in the 1700 years since its writing. Christians seldom dare open ourselves up this way.

Christian writing in general is rarely so raw and poignant. We usually write of our victories, firmly-held doctrines and glorious past. To write of our own pain and sin is dangerous, because it exposes us to the attacks of critics, even from our own Christian world. To be so glaringly genuine demands a willingness to be attacked or even mocked. In this present day, some of the most vocal critics are our own, who are more than willing to bury a brother in Christ if it means that they can stand on the tomb to climb higher in their own journey. Thus, most Christian books are guarded, careful and safe.

You hold in your hands a book of rare courage. It is neither safe nor guarded. It is a call to arms. Joe Donahue has written a book that can literally change your life.

Like Augustine, Joe has peeled back the layers of his life, so the reader can find the peace he has found. The method of his writing, however, is to take the reader on a journey through his abused childhood and upbringing. I have not read many books that have kept me up at night. urgent is one of them.

The author's passion for the lost, hell-bound world is evident on every page. Yet the remarkable thing about this book is the application of that passion. Like Augustine in many ways, Joe Donahue is a careful exegete. He unpacks the Scripture, such as his vivid retelling of the encounter between Jesus and Bartimaeus. Yet behind every carefully-chosen word you can feel Joe's empathy. He is not simply telling a story. He writes as one who has encountered Christ like Bartimaeus…

Like all of us, Bartimaeus was a broken and grief-stricken soul. Most of us would secretly identify with this blind man who cried out to Christ. We would privately state that we can understand his tears and sorrow. We might even preach a sermon or teach a lesson that would draw parallels between our own history and that of this brother healed by our Lord.

Yet Joe Donahue does something far more daring.

He draws back the curtain and tells his story in such a way that you know—beyond any doubt— that he knows Bartimaeus' desperation. It infuses his writing on virtually every page.

If it sounds to you like I was moved by this book, then GOOD. That is precisely what I am trying to convey. I have been blessed to live a life that allows me to read a myriad of books, both theological in nature and practical in content. For the most part, evangelical Christian books are an encouragement to my soul, or at least engaging. They point me to Jesus Christ and call me to deeper holiness.

Yet few books *touch me.*

Perhaps this is my own sinful failing, or the by-product of a busy life. Yet few books seize my attention in such a way that I cannot put them down. I finished my first read-through of this book during one evening, and when I glanced up to the clock on my nightstand, it was 3:00 a.m. I had been unaware that I had been reading through the midnight hours. Joe Donahue has not written a book to just entertain you. He has written a book to challenge you to the core.

The central theme of urgency is clear. Time is short, as is our opportunity to tell others about Christ. Joe weaves that common theme throughout. Yet like Paul before King Agrippa in Acts 26, he uses his testimony to draw us to act on this conviction. We all share a common ticking clock, and we all share in a common encounter with the risen Lord. This should change us. Obviously, it has changed Joe.

Thus, this is more than just a recommendation, or a suggestion. This is more than just an endorsement. This is a challenge. Read this book carefully. Read this book, and I dare you to remain unmoved. You may wince through some of Joe's most moving confessions, but I do not believe you can remain unaffected by them.

Joe has written a book that is both theologically profound, and emotionally pulsating. This is a book for both students and teachers. This book is theology with a heartbeat. I pray that God releases him to write many more books like this one. We desperately need more men like Augustine and Joe Donahue, who are willing to expose their wounds so others can find the healing power of Jesus.

Ergun Mehmet Caner, D.Theol.
Liberty University
Lynchburg, Virginia

Dedication

I am so grateful that Jesus Christ has saved me. I have been made new. I have been born twice. The first time I was born into sin. The second time I was born forgiven through his death and resurrection.

Then to top off my salvation, he gave me my wife Kristy. Kristy is my encourager, my motivator, and my love. We are one, and she loves me completely.

Thank you Kristy for your patience, grace and unending love you have for me. You are an incredible wife, a godly mother and a Christ-honoring example to our three little girls. Your stunning beauty radiates from the inside, out.

Then, God entrusted to Kristy and myself, Sofia, Naomi, and my little Violet born just a few weeks before this book went to print. Three little girls, age three and under, whom we pray one day, will also be born again.

Joe Donahue

chapter 1

urgent:

a personal matter

The Background

I grew up the oldest son out of a family of six children.

We lived in a small, two-bedroom trailer in the mountains of southwestern Pennsylvania. All six of us kids slept in a bedroom in the back of the trailer.

Six kids. One room. No beds.

My bed consisted of a spot on the floor in the closet. I had my sleeping bag and some old blankets for a pillow. No carpeting. Just plywood.

The plywood floor ran throughout the trailer. When Dad would come home late at night from drinking in the bars, I could hear him. I might not hear the door open up, but I could hear his boots walking on that plywood floor.

Are those steps coming back here, or are they going the other way? Was he coming back to us?

Dad was an alcoholic. He had a volatile temper.

Mom would cook a meal for Dad, and if she did not pre-pare it correctly, my dad would fling the plate down the hallway. He would curse, scream at her, and the food would splatter everywhere.

There was always an episode of anger. Every week.

If he reached for a glass to pour his beer into and it was still dirty, that was usually the trigger for another episode of anger.

Maybe if he stepped on a Lego.

Or the bike was not put up.

Or the dog dish was empty.

Or the wood was not chopped.

Or the grass was not cut.

Or the chickens had not been fed.

Any chore or task left incomplete, or finished incorrectly, usually led to another nightmare in our home.

Regardless of school the next morning, anytime of night he would scream us awake.

If one unwashed dish remained in the skink, all the plates, cups, bowls, silverware, and every cooking utensil in the house, would have to be washed, dried, and put back in the cabinets.

All the while, Dad would be raging and hurling insults at us:

You are pathetic.

You are worthless.

You are an idiot.

You are stupid.

But most names I cannot print.

So the story went. Day after day. Night after night. Week after week. Minute after minute.

The Day of Death

We raised chickens. I guess most poor families do. Eggs and chicken meat were regular staples in our home.

Before the sun had risen, a rooster crowed repeatedly beside Dad's bedroom window. That rooster received the unflinching, drunken fury of my still-drunk-from-the-night-before dad.

Dad grabbed his bow and arrow, slid the window open, and shot that red rooster right through the chest. He missed the heart. With one wing flapping, and the other wing pinned to his breast the rooster fled into the hills.

Go find it.

We never found it.

But the rest of that day, Dad sentenced most of the chickens to death.

He stood on the porch, with a sling of arrows and an outstretched bow in his hand, aimed, shot, and killed every chicken that came into his line of vision.

Flopping and flapping, the chickens ran around in circles until they dropped dead. Then, we chopped off their heads with a hatchet, drained the blood, and plucked their feathers.

Mom chopped them up and stuck them in the freezer. We ate chicken throughout the year.

We never did find that rooster though.

The Target

I was around eight years old.

One evening at dusk, he was shooting a rifle along the front porch down the side of the trailer.

The target? An old hubcap in the center of the hayfield that backed up to our trailer.

He told me to go check the target to see if he had hit it.

No.

Do it, you cry-baby.

I will never forget the feeling that I had walking across the hay field with my back to him. Little hairs stood up on the back of my neck. Goosebumps raced all over my body.

Would he shoot me in the back? Would he kill me like the chickens? Was I as useless as the chickens were to him?

I cried all the way to the target and back to my dad with the news; he missed the target with every shot.

You sissy. Go get me a beer.

I was like the chicken. Nothing more than a target for his temper.

The Secret

Sexual abuse occurred in many ways over the years of my childhood.

Groping me.

Rubbing me.

Making me do things to him.

He showed me pornographic videos at night when my other brothers and sisters were asleep, and made me sit very close to him while he touched me.

I carried secret shame for a very long time.

The Rage

One night, Dad came home from the bars dead drunk.

I pretended to be asleep in the closet in my sleeping bag on the floor.

I heard dishes breaking against the wall in the kitchen. Silverware splattering. Glass shattering. Metal clanging. Wood splitting.

I laid on the floor thinking:

God, please do not let him come back here next.

Most of the night, I heard my mom crying.

I wanted to say something to my brothers and sisters, but I was so afraid that even a whisper would bring my dad back there, and whatever was going on out there in the kitchen would begin to happen back there with us.

A knot of fear began to grip my heart. It felt like a hand was inside my chest, squeezing my heart.

I could not breathe, but I was breathing.

Mom continued sobbing, and the crashing noises grew more furious. Dad was screaming. Mom was crying. Things were being smashed.

At some point in the early morning hours, I fell asleep.

When I woke up for school the next morning, I walked to the kitchen entrance, and it looked like a bomb had gone off. Chairs slammed down through the kitchen floor. Knives thrown through the wall. The cabinets were knocked over. Food was everywhere. Cereal was everywhere. Bags of flour, sugar, coffee had been ripped open and layered the kitchen.

The refrigerator was flipped over on its back. The milk, juice, and beer spread across the floor. The dishes were smashed and destroyed. They were thrown out in the yard. The kitchen table had been broken in half.

Dad was passed out in the living room, and a Johnny Cash record was skipping on the record player.

Mom sat weeping in the center of this mess, with a broom and a dustpan. I remember thinking at that point:

Mom looks like a little wilted flower, ready to give up. Ready to quit struggling to live.

I went to school that day and I remember my mom saying:

Do not say anything about what happened.

I kept my mouth shut.

I was used to pretending that my life was amazing. I pretended to have the best dad in the world. The best family in the world. Nobody knew what happened in my home. I hid the drinking. The names. The sexual abuse. All that junk disappeared the moment the bus appeared around the corner of the road.

The Hero

One afternoon I got off the school bus as usual and began the walk up our long dirt driveway. As I got closer to the trailer, I heard Mom screaming from inside her bedroom.

My mom was screaming. She was weeping. She was battling my dad.

As I stepped into the trailer, her muffled cries became so much clearer.

No! Ed. Please Stop! No!

A part of me always wanted to be a hero. I wanted to step up to stop him. I wanted to stand up to Dad all the time and say:

Hey! Stop being so mean. Stop calling us names. Stop drinking beer. Stop touching me.

But the larger part of me lived in total fear of Dad. That part that lived in fear is what controlled me most of the time.

I knew I wanted to stop whatever was going on behind the bedroom door. I wanted to kick down the door and rescue my mom.

I walked over to their bedroom door, stretched my little eight-year-old hand out, and tried to grab the doorknob. I pulled back in fear and backed away.

I crossed over to the other side of the living room, sweating, pacing back and forth. Again, I reached back to the door. I wanted to open it so badly. I wanted Mommy to be safe. I could hear her just on the other side, screaming out and crying, "No! No! No!"

I paced the floor and beads of sweat covered my arms and

ran down my back. Silent tears streamed down my face. I pulled my hand back, like a chicken, and shrank away.

Finally, I grabbed the doorknob and turned it just a bit, and gave the door a little push. Dad was naked on top of mom. Mom was naked, fighting, and pushing against drunken strength.

He was raping her.

I stood there silently for what felt like hours, but must have been only seconds. Mom saw me standing in the room. While Dad forced himself on her, and she continued to resist, she looked at me with eyes of pain, sorrow, regret and fear, but said nothing. She tried to pull the blanket up to cover her naked body.

Dad turned his head to follow her gaze. He pointed his finger in my face and said:

Go get the knife.

As a kid, there was always a knife I could not touch. I called it, *the knife.*

Go get the knife.

My mom immediately began to say, "No! No! No!"

Holding Mom down with one hand, Dad kept ordering me:

Go get the knife!

I shrank away. The hero I wanted to be, left. I backed away
and turned to go into the kitchen. The further I made it
toward the kitchen, with each step; Mom's cry of *no*, pen-
etrated deeper into my heart.

I opened the kitchen drawer. There is *the knife*, and beside
it is a butter knife. I grabbed the butter knife and held it in
my hand.

I saw what he was doing to Mom. And I did not want him
to turn on me, too. But I did not want him to cut her either.

I brought the butter knife to my dad and held it out to him
with the same little hand that opened the door to rescue
mom. He called me names, knocked the knife out of my
hand, slammed the door, and finished raping her.

I stood outside the door and cried.

Some hero.

While my dad destroyed our family, cancer began to destroy
Dad's body. He had cancer it in his lymph nodes. It was
Hodgkin's disease. It was spreading quickly. For the first
time ever, he was scared.

He quit drinking.

No beer. No whiskey. No liquor. No alcohol. He began

attending meetings for the local chapter of Alcoholics Anonymous.

He underwent surgery. Thankfully, the cancer was removed from his body, and it went into remission. Grateful for a second chance at life, he promised a new life, a new family—because his drinking days were over.

The New Life

In moments of remorse over the abuse and violence, Dad would make statements like:

This is my last beer. I am not going to drink anymore.

I understand what it is doing to you kids. I am not going to drink anymore.

So he would proudly drink his last beer, and the following night he was drinking his "last beer" again… and the next night he was having his "last beer" again.

Always broken promises:

Joe, I am going to show up at your T-ball game today.

He never did. I would be standing in the outfield, waiting to see my dad pulling up in our old Buick, but I never saw him there.

I began to stop hoping, because I hated to be disappointed.

But every time he said he was going to quit drinking, man, I believed he was going to quit drinking. I believed it with all my heart.

And this time—after cancer—he quit drinking! That began the best times of my childhood!

He would come out in the yard and play kick-ball with us. He built a big snow fort in our driveway in Pennsylvania.

Then he made another promise: A new life.

We packed up everything we owned in that two-bedroom trailer, loaded it onto an old school bus, and moved to Tennessee.

A new life. A new house. A new start. No more drinking. No more temper. No more abuse. No more fighting. No more yelling.

We were so ready for this new life. But it never happened.

The abuse began again. The drinking began again—the fighting, the tempers, the fear, the worry, the covering up. There was no new life. Life was just the old life with a mask on. There was nothing new. Nothing had changed within my dad. In order for something to be made new, it needs to be transformed on the inside first.

My dad made a promise of the new life, but the DNA of our home never changed. The old life was there, and it was worse than before. I fought with my brothers and sisters. We screamed and tore into one another daily. We blamed each other for what was going on in our home. We beat each other up. We ganged up on each other.

We lived out the anger and frustration we had in our hearts…the hate, the bitterness, the accusations, the lying.

All this hate, abuse and torment… the result of one man.

But that man was not my dad.

It was Adam.

You see, God created us to have a relationship with Him. Genesis 2:7 says:

And the Lord God formed man of the dust of the ground, and breathed into his nostrils the breath of life; and man became a living being. Genesis 2:7, NLT

In the book of Genesis, we see God walking with Adam from place to place in the Garden of Eden. We see God having a relationship with Adam and Eve, walking with them and talking with them. We see Him being there with them. They knew God's voice. They knew intimate fellowship with the Father like none other, yet they still chose to sin. They knew complete love and closeness with the Creator of the galaxies—and rebelled against Him.

When Adam chose to rebel against his Creator in the Garden of Eden, his decision had serious consequences that pitched all of humanity into sin.

Romans 5:12 says:

When Adam sinned, sin entered the world. Adam's sin brought death because everyone sinned. Romans 5:12, NLT

The old life, the old sin, that heartbreaking life I lived as a child is not the result of my father. Is he responsible? Absolutely. But the truth is, it was because of sin. It is because of sin that ran rampant in my father's heart. It is because sin ran rampant in my family's lives.

This thing called sin is nasty. This thing called sin is absolutely the worst thing we could possibly imagine, and that is why it repulses God so much. God is Holy, pure, righteous, and just.

One reason sin is so offensive to God is because He knows the damage it does.

The Shame

In seventh grade, I was sitting in class when the intercom buzzed and the voice on the other end asked me to come to the office. I walked into the office, and saw the principal, a teacher, and a few other people. They began questioning me, personal questions, about what was going on in my home. They told me they had received a report from somebody, and they wanted to know what was going on.

Nothing. Nothing is going on.

Everything is great. Everything is perfect. Why are you asking these questions? My home life is great.

Even though I had an opportunity to escape, even though there was a chance for me to say:

Yes! Let me tell you about what was going on.

I did not say a word about the abuse or the drinking.

I had two things that kept me in denial. The first, I still had that hero thing. I wanted to protect my dad. I loved my dad despite the abuse. I loved him. I hated what he did, but I loved him.

There was also another reason. I was *so ashamed.* I was ashamed of what was going on in my home. I was the oldest son and I was not doing anything to prevent it. I was not protecting my siblings. I was no hero.

I was so ashamed that my dad was sexually abusing me, a male. And all the jokes that would develop from that. There was simply no way I would ever tell anybody. I imagined people teasing me the rest of my life. Men would call me all kinds of names.

The best thing for me to do was to lie. Keep my mask on,

and fight anybody that tried to take it off.

The Phone Call

I used to dream I could fly.

In my dreams, I would take a few bounding steps, and leap into the air. The next thing I knew, I was flying.

I would fly above my family. Above my house. Out of the reach of Dad. The moment I had an opportunity to escape from his reach, I rejected it.

My mom showed up at school one day and told me to turn in my books; we were leaving. That afternoon we drove to Nashville, Tennessee to a place called the YWCA shelter for battered and abused families.

It was a large house. It had many rooms for women and their children who had been beaten and abused.

This house made me extremely uncomfortable. I liked my mask and as long as I was going to school and pretending everything was okay, then nobody knew anything. Now, I was in a house where everybody who was living there, was there because of a similar reason. Something was not right at home.

At school, I did not have to face what I faced every night at home. Now, in the shelter, I had to face the fact my dad was not a good dad, and our life would never be the same. That really scared me to death.

I ran away from the shelter after convincing them that I wanted a ticket to visit a friend in Kentucky. I called my dad as soon as I could.

A couple of days later my dad sent me back to the shelter. The people at the shelter were upset with me. They were afraid I told dad their secret location...the place where the shelter was. They wanted me to see a psychiatrist to help me deal with the anger.

After initial refusal, they drove me to a hospital and the doors locked behind me as I walked in. A place called Vanderbilt Child and Adolescent Psychiatric Hospital. A place for teenagers who had a rough past like mine... teenagers who had maybe been in trouble with the law, or teenagers who had been abused as children.

I stayed there for three months, alone, away from my family, not knowing what was going on in the outside world. Rarely did I get a visit from my mom. Rarely did I get to see my brothers and sisters while I was there.

At the end of three months in the psychiatric hospital, I was told that I could not live with my mom because I was too much trouble and she could not afford me. I went to live with Nana.

I lived with Nana for about a year before I spoke to my dad again. Dad had moved to Florida, and was living in an old camper in the Ocala National Forest.

Dad called on the phone to let me know he was going to drive up to visit. I remember talking with him as I held that phone receiver to my ear. I did not know what to say. A lump swelled up in my throat. I could not speak. The people at the shelter told me Dad was a bad person. They told me not to talk to him, not to communicate with him. The people at the hospital told me Dad was a bad person and told me not to communicate with him. But he was my dad.

As my dad's voice flowed over the line, I listened to him. My hands were shaking. I wanted to talk to him...but that lump grew larger in my throat. It had been about two years since I saw him last.

He said:

Did they tell you not to talk to me? Did they tell you I was a bad person?

Yes. My voice cracked.

Dad told me:

I am sorry I put you kids through this, and I am going to be coming up to visit with you soon.

I could not talk. The lump in my throat felt as though it was going to burst. I handed Nana the phone and she told him it was not a really a good time to come up and visit.

I made an escape outside and cried.

A few weeks later, Dad called Nana again. From the hall-way, I listened as my Nana talked with him. She said:

It is back? The cancer? Well how bad is it? How much time do they say you have? Two weeks?

I listened and I heard my dad was going to die in just a couple of weeks. It just shattered me. I cried into my pillow all night long knowing I was not going to see my dad again.

The Handcuffs

The police officer glared at my dad and ordered him to put his hands behind his back as he handcuffed him. He point-ed at me.

Look at what you are doing to him.

Tears streamed down my face.

I was fifteen years old. I had just driven my drunken dad from Nana's house in Bumpus Mills, Tennessee to the VA Hospital in Nashville.

No driver's license.

No permit.

Never driven on the interstate before...and driving an old black Chevrolet Custom Deluxe pickup truck through the streets of Nashville.

Drunk as he could be and still standing, Dad had made the decision that he wanted to check in to the detoxification center of the VA Hospital in Nashville, Tennessee. Of course, I was his driver.

I drove the truck, with Dad in the passenger seat, for three hours. We made it through the traffic, the interstates, the roads, and parked in the parking lot of the VA Hospital.

As we left the truck, he tucked a pint of Kentucky Bourbon into the back of his pants under his shirttail, and he stumbled into the administration wing of the VA hospital.

A nurse spotted the whiskey bottle, and called security. It was a federal crime to bring alcohol onto government property. Even though he was requesting admittance to the detoxification program, he was arrested and spent the next 48 hours in jail.

That was one way to dry him out.

When I picked him up from the jail two days later, his eyes were black, and his false teeth were cracked in two. I guess somebody did not like what he was saying.

The Savior

I spent my high school years picking on people who were smaller than I was and running from the people who were bigger than I was. I could make teachers laugh. I was the class clown. It seemed that everybody really liked me. Why? Because I was great at wearing that mask. I was great at hiding my heart. I was great at not showing the world who I really was or what I had really gone through in my life.

After I graduated from High School in Dover, Tennessee, I immediately began to work as a laborer on a brick crew.

Roughly three weeks after I graduated, a girl named Cyndi invited me to go to church with her on a Wednesday night for youth group.

I visited her youth group on a Wednesday night. Around 25-35 teenagers were sitting in a circle, Bibles open, and there was a youth pastor there. His name was Robbie. Robbie was teaching them the Word of God, and they were listening, really listening. They were leaning forward in their seats. They were asking questions.

I had never been around people studying the Bible before.

Suddenly, I felt something I had never felt in my life. I felt a light in my heart, a warmness. Drawing me to listen intently to what was being said.

Even though I grew up Catholic, I was never interested in the things of God. Yet here was this whole group of kids, and they were talking about God as if they knew Him. That blew my mind.

I went back the following Wednesday. Then again the next

Wednesday. I began to attend church on Sundays. Then
Sunday evenings.

One night another girl came up to me. She was sweating,
and she wanted to ask me a question. She began to explain
to me about Jesus, about how Jesus died on the cross to set
us free from sin.

I really did not comprehend how I was supposed to respond
to that message, and she stepped out of the room to get
Robbie.

Robbie entered the room, looked me in the eye and said:

I hear you want to know more about Jesus.

Yes, I do.

The warm light in my heart was now a roaring fire.

The fire was drawing me to listen, to cling to the words he
shared with me.

Robbie explained from Paul's letter to the Romans that "all
have sinned and fall short of the glory of God."

Do you understand, Joe, that you are a sinner?

Hello, yes. I understand I am a sinner.

Okay, it is not just you. It is myself. It is everybody.

He showed me Romans 6:23. "The wages of sin is death, but the gift of God is eternal life through Christ Jesus."

Joe, do you understand the Bible says that the penalty for your sin, what you get in return for your sin is eternal separation from God?

Gulp.

"Yes. That is big. Yes, I understand it is clicking in my head. It's clicking in my heart."

Do you understand Christ died on the cross to set you free from sin? Christ died on the cross to offer you forgiveness. Christ died on the cross to pay the penalty for you. It is a substitute. He died in your place so you would not have to pay the penalty for sin.

He showed me several passages of scripture that evening. The following verses spoke clearly to me:

For Christ has suffered once for sins the just for the unjust that He might bring us to God, being put to death in the flesh but made alive by the Spirit." 1 Peter 3:18, NLT

But to as many as received Him, to them He gave the right to become children of God, to those who believe in His name. John 1:12, NLT

Then he showed me Romans 10:9 that says, "If you confess with your mouth Jesus is Lord and you believe in your heart that God has raised Him from the dead, you will be saved."

Joe, do you want to accept Christ right now?

Man, you bet I do!

Do you want to pray after me, or do you just want to pray on your own?

I will pray on my own.

I got down on my knees beside an old couch in his office, and I prayed:

Jesus, I understand you died on the cross for me. I confess to you that I am a sinner. I confess to you that the penalty for my sin is eternal separation from you. I understand you have died to set me free, and Jesus I ask that you would come into my life. I ask that you would come into my heart. I ask You to save me from my sin and give me this new life. And Jesus that You would walk with me, that that You would hold my hand the rest of my life. Jesus, I want to know you like I see all the rest of these teenagers who know you. I want to know you for the rest of my life.

I lifted up my head and opened my eyes. I did not know what to expect next. I had watched televangelists before, and thought Robbie was about to smack me on the head. The smack never came.

The new me stood up, and the old me never raised from that spot.

Inside my heart, I felt like I could walk like I had never walked before. I felt like if I jumped off the ground, I would never land back on the ground. I felt like I could fly.

The burden I had been carrying for years, this burden of sin—the burden of shame—was gone.

I had never even realized it was there. But when it was gone, I experienced freedom.

Looking back, I see very clearly what happened to me in that moment. Jesus literally made me new on the inside... from the inside out. He came in and He annihilated my old life and gave me a brand new life.

Jesus gave me a brand new life. I was changed. I was different.

That new life can happen to you, too.

I was new. Not because I felt new. I *was* new. Things had changed deep within. I was transformed.

Therefore, if anyone is in Christ, he is a new creation; old things have passed away; behold, all things have become new.
2 Corinthians 5:17, NLT

The Death of my Father

In 1993, two years after I prayed that prayer and was saved, God brought me to a place in which I knew I needed to forgive Dad.

I wrote him a letter. While I was writing that letter to him, God gave me the peace to forgive him. In the letter, I explained in detail exactly what I was forgiving him for. I spelled it out in detailed bullet points.

Dad I forgive you for sexually abusing me.

I forgive you for calling me these names (and I would write out the names).

I forgive you for drinking all the time.

I forgive you for all the broken promises.

I forgive you for raping Mom.

The list went on and on. I wanted to make sure he understood that years of drinking and abuse hurt me. I wasn't casually saying, "Don't worry about it."

I wanted to make sure he knew I remembered, and even though I remembered, I wanted to show the forgiveness of Christ and say, "I remember, but I'm forgiving you because I love you, and I'm not holding it against you anymore."

I knew my dad did not deserve forgiveness, but I also knew, neither did I. If Jesus, who is perfect and suffered in my place on the cross could forgive me for my sin, then who am I to hold my father's sin against him and not be forgiving of him?

Dad wrote a letter back to me:

Joe, I just want you to thank you for your letter and thank you for forgiving me because I knew that if you kids could forgive me for what I did to you, you could move on with life and God would bring you peace.

I watched Dad die five years later.

I was 25 years old and I was at his bedside when he died in the VA Hospital in Florida. I held his hand, and I reminded him as he was drawing his last breaths:

Remember Dad, I forgive you. I am not holding anything against you. And I want you to understand something. You can trust Jesus Christ to be your Lord and Savior.

His eyes were closed. He had breathing tubes in his mouth. He had all kinds of tubes hooked up to him. His breathing was raspy as he was drawing just his last breaths.

I kept holding his hand.

Dad I want you to know that Jesus will forgive you. Right now. I know you can hear me. Even right now, you can accept Christ

as your Savior. Do you understand that, Dad? Do you under-
stand there is an eternal hell waiting for you if you do not? Dad,
I love you.

My dad died a few minutes later.

Until I enter heaven, I will never know if he trusted Christ
to be his Lord and Savior.

God has brought healing to me, but the most important
thing is God gave me new life through forgiving me for my
sin. It is because God forgave me for my sin that I was able
to forgive my dad. It is because God forgave me of my sin
that I am able to stand before crowds today; I am able to
stand before men and say.

My dad sexually abused me, and I forgave him because of the
new life I have been given in Christ.

Do you understand how humbling that is?

Do you know how many times I refused to go into ministry,
how many times I refused God's call to speak and to share
my testimony because I was so ashamed of it?

Today, I am a man unashamed of my past, because I am
new.

I have been seeking to walk with Jesus since 1991. I was the
first person in my family to graduate from high school. I
was the first person in my family to graduate from college.

While I was in college, I chose to double major. One major was in my area of study. The other major was for God.

I read my Bible daily.

I would sit at the feet of Jesus for 2-3 hours in the morning in my dorm room before heading out for the day. I wanted all that Jesus wanted me to experience.

In 1996, I surrendered to God's call to ministry.

In 1999, I married Kristy, the pastor's daughter of the church I was saved in. I have been serving in ministry since 1993, and we have been serving together in ministry since 1998. We have two sweet precious daughters and one more on the way at the writing of this book.

You know why?

It is because the night I trusted Jesus Christ to be my Savior, the old Joe never stood up.

I have been blessed with peace and joy. I have been blessed with an ability to forgive and to share the love of Jesus Christ with others. I have been richly blessed with two sweet little girls who climb into my lap, who love me, and trust me. I have been blessed with a wife who serves with me as a friend, a motivator, and my lover.

The old Joe never stood up.

I want you to experience new life in Christ. I want you to experience that hope in Christ. That newness of life. The forgiveness of sin. The old life is a thing of the past.

That night, Robbie, my youth pastor told me about Jesus, he did not know I was abused as a kid. He did not know my dad was an alcoholic.

He did not need to know.

He understood everything he needed to know:

I was a human, therefore I was a sinner, and I needed Jesus Christ to be my Lord and Savior. I needed to be forgiven for my sins.

We all do.

Even you.

chapter 2

urgent cry

Sofie, my three-year-old, is an extremely meticulous eater. She has one of the most sensitive gag reflexes in the world. Peas make her gag. Her first taste of ice cream made her gag. Chocolate makes her gag. She gags on anything she attempts to eat for the first time.

It was not because we never presented her with a variety of food. Kristy, her mom, stuffed the grocery carts with all types of whole foods, organic foods, and smashed it all together to give her a variety.

It all made her gag.

When Kristy first began introducing those new foods to her—her gag reflex would kick in, her tongue would poke out, her face would scrunch together…it was a cute little face…but very frustrating at times. On her one-year-old birthday, she was introduced to butter cream icing. Every child's dream, right?

Alas, she gagged.

Now that Sofie is three years of age, the gag reflex has evolved into the words, "I don't like it."

Try this cinnamon roll.

I don't like it.

Eat your veggies.

I don't like it.

Eat your meat.

I don't like it.

I know one day it will get better.

But, spaghetti and meatballs has quickly become the house favorite. Sofia loves spaghetti and meatballs. It is the best stuff that has ever been served from the Donahue dinner table.

One particular night, Sofie ate one whole plate of this magic pasta dish. Then asked for seconds...then thirds! Kristy and I were so excited to see her eating; we kept piling up her plate. More? Sure!

Later, it was time for bed. Since babies, we have always given them a sippy cup of milk to take with them to their bed.

We learned a very important lesson that night.

Milk and three plates of pasta do not mix well in a little tummy.

Forty-five minutes after Sofie went to sleep, she spewed

everywhere. Naturally, she was lying on her back, and like a geyser, a milky red spaghetti and meatball mixture launched from her mouth and up into the nightlight air. It cascaded down into her hair, trickled into her ears, and soaked the sheets, the pillow, the bed, and Curious George.

For the next hour, nothing else mattered except to get Sofie into the tub, change the sheets, clean the carpet, wash Curious George, and tuck her back into bed. I had other things that I had been doing—but nothing else mattered anymore.

The only thing that mattered was hugging her to ease her heart from sobbing, bathing her, washing the yuck away, and bringing comfort to her.

The television was not important. Writing was not important. Cleaning the house was not important. The only thing that mattered in that moment was taking care of Sofie. Her needs, the need to be cleaned became urgent.

When you think about your relationship to God, does the word urgent come to your mind?

When it comes to you and God, can it be said that being in his presence and becoming more like our loving God is the only thing that matters? Are you urgent about living in his presence?

Maybe you are, and maybe you are not.

The sense of urgency can only occur when a greater need surfaces that is more pressing and more significant than anything else swirling in your life.

Have you ever stopped to consider that the most important need in your life, the most urgent need in your life, is to be in God's presence on a regular basis?

Your wife needs you to be in God's presence.

Your husband needs you to be in God's presence.

Your family. Your children. Your co-workers. They need you to shine the light of Christ, to be the hands and feet of Jesus. So your most pressing need, your most urgent need, is to rest in God's presence to be filled with his light and love.

And gentleness.

And compassion.

And forgiveness.

And grace.

And mercy.

And kindness.

And patience.

And when you are spending time in his presence, you are having a God-sized, meteor-like impact deep in the hearts of those around you.

Instead of retaliating, you forgive.

Instead of spouting off words you do not mean, you smile a genuine smile.

Instead of treating others harshly, you show grace and compassion.

These actions are not forced. They are spilling out of you naturally because you are spending time with Jesus. Your world needs you to spill and ooze out the Spirit of the Living God, because our world is broken and is in need of a Savior.

In this chapter, let us examine a passage of scripture that portrays a man urgently seeking Jesus to meet his need. I think you will discover, as I have, that this man, Bartimaeus can become one of the greatest teachers and influencers of all time.

Read the following passage carefully. As you read it, circle the words that describe Bartimaeus' needs.

And so they reached Jericho. Later, as Jesus and his disciples left town, a great crowd was following. A blind beggar named Bartimaeus (son of Timaeus) was sitting beside the road as Jesus was going by. When Bartimaeus heard that Jesus from Nazareth was nearby, he began to shout out, "Jesus, Son of

6

*David, have mercy on me!" "Be quiet!" some of the people yelled
at him. But he only shouted louder, "Son of David, have mercy
on me!" When Jesus heard him, he stopped and said, "Tell him to
come here." So they called the blind man. "Cheer up," they said.
"Come on, he's calling you!" Bartimaeus threw aside his coat,
jumped up, and came to Jesus. "What do you want me to do for
you?" Jesus asked. "Teacher," the blind man said, "I want to see!"
And Jesus said to him, "Go your way. Your faith has healed you."
And instantly the blind man could see! Then he followed Jesus
down the road. Mark 10:46-52, NLT*

Bartimaeus was blind. Because of his blindness, he was
forced to beg for money and food. Because he was blind, a
certain social stigma preceded him wherever he went. He
was blind, because, well he or his parents must have committed an act so vile, so disgusting that God punished him
with blindness.

Wherever he traveled. Wherever he sat to beg. With every
word, he cried out. With every hushed whisper of his name.

He was a nobody. He was a nothing. He was an after-
thought. He was a drop-off place for table scraps. He was
the epitome of a useless life. He could do nothing but beg.
He had nothing to live for except his next few bites of food.
He had nobody to live for. Who would marry a blind beggar?

Because of his blindness, he was worthless.

His social standing was similar to those with leprosy. He
was an outcast.

It should also be noted, that blindness was not the only thing that Bartimaeus had going against him. Nope. Blindness was not the only struggle for Bartimaeus.

He also had family issues that stemmed from his dad. His dad was known in the community for doing something bad. Really bad.

Bartimaeus' name defined is "Son of Timaeus." Timaeus was the name for Bartimaeus' dad. Timaeus' name has a tragic definition: "Defiled." We do not know why Timaeus was branded a defiled man, but unfortunately the poor decisions his dad had made, followed him around.

When somebody even whispered the name of poor Bartimaeus, they were reminding Bartimaeus that his daddy was trash, and so was he. When they shooed him away from the entrance to their home, or swept him like dirt from the entrance to their shop, they were merely cleaning defiled trash from the streets.

Even his name hurt him.

Not only was Bartimaeus a perversion of life, but he was also the son of a man who was "defiled."

It seemed like life had taken a big old garbage bag and dropped it right on the head of Bartimaeus.

Beggars slept in the cold. They slept in the rain. In the heat. In the wind. In the thunderstorms. Few had families because of the social stigma. They begged for food just to get by…and to top it off, this beggar was blind.

I imagine his thought life went something like this:

If I had my sight, I could work. If I could work, I could earn money and not beg for food. If my eyes worked, maybe I could have a wife, and a family. If I had my sight, I would not be treated like trash…like a nobody.

If I could see, maybe I could do something great!

Are you feeling sorry for Bartimaeus yet? It gets worse.

In fact, it is quite possible that Bartimaeus knew what it was like to see! At the end of this passage of scripture when he tells Jesus what he wants, he uses the Greek word Anablepō. Strong's Exhaustive Concordance defines the word this way:

Anablepō: which means 'to see' or "to recover lost sight."

Now, I do not know about you. I know the old adage claims, "It is better to have loved and lost than to have never loved at all."

I do not think that saying has any merit here. To me, it is one thing to have never known what "sight" is. To lose the sense of vision, after having a dependency of mobilization and coordination would be far worse. Have you ever tried to walk around blindfolded? You will stumble, and bump, and crawl if you feel as though you are in an unsafe environment.

Imagine you will never see again. Imagine you have lost your independence. Imagine you have been reduced to begging on the streets for food because of your blindness. Your loved ones have left you. You have nothing. You have been stripped of any dignity you had before.

Sin has robbed you and stolen your ability to see.

When we think about sin, we often think about it in the context of something that we choose to do. We understand that sin separates us from God, but we forget how much we have lost because of sin.

Sin traps us. Spiritual sin can become a physical habit or an addiction. One sin leads to another sin. It is a cycle that you find yourself powerless against. Often times, parental sins are passed down to younger generations. If your parents come from a broken home, with cheating and lying and fighting, chances are you will be doing those same things when you begin a family. Sin leads to sin leads to sin leads to sin. Its trapping power is respectful of nobody. We have seen many men and women trapped into sin's sticky web. Families have been shredded because of sin's trapping and paralyzing power.

Instead of the world and people growing better every moment, the world is growing worse and worse. Adam and Eve were created perfect, right and pure. They chose to sin, and since they sinned, sin spread to every person who has ever lived and as society continues to grow, we will continue to become less like God and more like sin. The further the world gets from the Garden of Eden, the further the World sinks into sin.

Sin teaches us to blame others when we mess up. Have you ever done something wrong, but blamed somebody else? Maybe you rationalize it in your mind so that you can justify it to others. "The reason I act the way I do is because my mom left....my dad left...no one loves me...That's why I act that way." Did something bad happen to you when you were a child that causes you to act the way you do?

Let me be honest with you. Speaking from the perspective as a childhood victim of sexual abuse from my alcoholic dad: *so what?* Are you going to let something that happened to you control you for the rest of your life? Seriously? Is it not time to accept responsibility for your own actions? We shift responsibility off our shoulders to blame somebody else because we think we will feel better. Instead, we just sink further into guilt and emptiness.

Sin develops insensitivity towards more sin. Like your fingertips develop calluses to protect them from wear and tear, your spirit and conscience will begin to erode towards sin. Those feelings of *Oh my gosh, this is wrong* will erode away like sand on the beach until you just do not care anymore. The flashes of shame on your cheek disappear and you grow emptier in your heart.

Do you sense an urgent need for Jesus yet? Sin is one mean and nasty puppy.

Sin has an ability to destroy you. As one gets used to a drug and wants something more, sin loses its ability to satisfy you. It becomes easier to sin without having a guilty conscience. Certain sins just do not satisfy you anymore. Gossip grows. Anger rages. You lash out at your family. You lose your temper at silly trivial things.

Hidden lust of the heart turns to the internet. Internet lusts turn to strip clubs. Families and marriages are destroyed for one more hit of sin. Just one more taste. Just one more whisper. Just one more hit. Just one more mean thing to say. Just one more night away from home. Sin's power over you grows to destroy you and everyone you love. Your arms twitch. Your eyes desire. Your heart aches to sin more and more and more.

Sin fans into flame the desire to be the best, regardless of the consequences. Sin makes us want and crave what somebody else has. The husband. The wife. The clothes. The hair. The body. We want the spot on the team. We want the job. We want the recognition. We want the car. We want the boyfriend. The girlfriend. The grades. The family. The parents. The money. The retirement accounts. The life.

Then, you grow so disgusted by yourself that you turn against your own body and begin to harm yourself. A few beers at the bar after work. Starving to look like the model. Having sex or sexual activity with others so you feel loved and accepted. Maybe you take a hit to get high to forget about your problems. Sin is committed to help you feel better about yourself, only to find yourself avoiding eye contact with the mirror image and feeling worse than you ever have felt before! Sin is nasty.

Do you sense an urgent need for Jesus yet? Are you sick and tired of the weight of sin yet?

What is your urgent personal need as you read this book? If Jesus was passing by right now, and you could call out to him, what would be your urgent need?

Would you cry out to him for a job? For a home? For forgive-
ness? For something you lost?

When Bartimaeus called out, it must have been a heart-wrenching sight. The sound of years of brokenness. Years of isolation. Years of anguish. Years of insecurity. Years of wandering. Years of begging. Years of hunger. Years of scorn. Years of ridicule. Years of unemployment.

He did not just simply say in a loud voice:

"Jesus, Son of David, have mercy on me."

He cried it.

He screeched it.

He wept it.

He sobbed it.

Years of brokenness had finally intersected with the presence of Jesus.

Repeatedly he cried aloud. How do we know this? First, the scripture says in v. 47, "he began to shout out." If he had simply shouted it out one time, the scriptures would not have indicated that Mark, the author, was 'summing up' what Bartimaeus was shouting out. In fact, he cried out so loud and so frequently, the crowd began to get very annoyed with his shouting out.

How and what Bartimaeus cried out indicates his belief of who Jesus was and is today. When he cried out, he used a phrase that very few people outside the disciples of Jesus had used. He called him, the Son of David.

There is something greatly significant about this.

Look at what happened in the very beginning of Jesus' ministry:

When he came to the village of Nazareth, his boyhood home, he went as usual to the synagogue on the Sabbath and stood up to read the Scriptures. The scroll containing the messages of Isaiah the prophet was handed to him, and he unrolled the scroll to the place where it says: "The Spirit of the Lord is upon me, for he has appointed me to preach Good News to the poor. He has sent me to proclaim that captives will be released, that the blind will see, that the downtrodden will be freed from their oppressors, and that the time of the Lord's favor has come." He rolled up the scroll, handed it back to the attendant, and sat down. Everyone in the synagogue stared at him intently. Then he said, "This Scripture has come true today before your very eyes!" Luke 4:16-18 NLT

Jesus read the passage from the Prophet Isaiah and said—I am the one!

Somehow, some way, word had reached the ears of this blind beggar that Jesus made a claim to be the one that fulfilled Isaiah's prophecy.

Even though he had been trashed by the world, he was

able to connect the dots and see that the miracles of Jesus proved that He was indeed the Messiah, the Savior of the World.

He got it.

He understood that Jesus was the Miracle Worker. That He was the Messiah. And Jesus could change his life.

Maybe he waited along the road for the Savior to come by. Or maybe Jesus just happened to come by. Either way, the life of this Blind beggar intersected with Jesus the Christ.

Bartimaeus believed Jesus to be the Son of David. When he called Jesus "Son of David," he was stating his belief that Jesus was indeed the Messiah and that the Messiah could open his eyes and give him sight.

It was a cry of faith that could not be quenched. He had to call out. He had to cry out. He had to take that opportunity to cry out as Jesus was passing by.

Do you believe that Jesus is who he says he is? Do you believe he can forgive you of your sins? Do you believe he can give you a new life, a new start? Do you believe that He personally loves you?

Bartimaeus did. He believed. Because he believed, he called out to be restored by Jesus. And Jesus restored him.

Despite the people around him who to told him to be quiet,

he called out—chances are, he was being obnoxious—but when something is urgent, you call out.

In fact, the people around him tried to dissuade him from crying out. The people were so annoyed at the cry from Bartimaeus. They must have been so embarrassed. Here was the great Miracle-worker walking through their town, and this riff-raff, this trash, this little blind beggar was throwing off the vibe.

Maybe you are holding back from calling out to Jesus because you fear that people around you will be embarrassed. Maybe you are one who is supposed to have it all together. Maybe you are the one who everybody knows is hurting.

Do not hold back any longer. You have held back long enough!

Call out!

Call out to Jesus now!

He is here to meet your needs. To forgive your sin. To bring you peace. To break the addictions. To start over. Right here. Right now.

He will not reject you. Look at how he treated Bartimaeus.

Most people fear they will be rejected by God.

People say things like, "If I were to go to church, the walls would fall in on me."

We seem to lock up, shut down and freeze when it comes to being in the presence of the only one who will unconditionally love us.

Is that you?

Realize for just a second that Jesus is willing to accept you just as you are.

All of your sin. Your secrets. Your shame. He sees it all and loves you completely.

When Jesus heard him, he stopped and said, "Tell him to come here." So they called the blind man. "Cheer up," they said. "Come on, he's calling you!" Bartimaeus threw aside his coat, jumped up, and came to Jesus. Mark 10:49-50, NLT.

Jesus did not turn Bartimaeus away. He will not turn you away either. Even if everybody in your family has, he will not.

The cry of Bartimaeus stopped Jesus in his tracks. Your cry will stop Jesus in his tracks. Take a deeper look at the response of Jesus.

He called Bartimaeus to him. He let Bartimaeus, *Blind* Bartimaeus, stumble his way through the darkness to Jesus. His last few steps in the darkness.

The significance of this is overwhelming. Bartimaeus had
enough faith to cry out, but did he have enough faith to go
to Jesus?

Do you?

Do you have enough faith in Jesus to do something about
your condition? To tell a friend? To apologize to family?
That co-worker?

As he journeyed to Jesus, can you imagine what was going
through his mind? *These are the last few steps I will ever take
in darkness.*

*"What do you want me to do for you?" Jesus asked. "Teacher,"
the blind man said, "I want to see!" And Jesus said to him, "Go
your way. Your faith has healed you." And instantly the blind man
could see! Then he followed Jesus down the road.*
Mark 10:51-52, NLT

Jesus said to him, "What do you want me to do for you?"

It seems obvious that Jesus knew the needs of this man.
Jesus asked this of Bartimaeus, to clarify something in the
mind of Bartimaeus. Was he really prepared to have his life
transformed? Was he ready to be changed? To begin a new
life? To break old habits?

The truth is, some people do not really want to be changed.
A prayer for them? Certainly! But not real healing. They are
comfortable with their problems and have entered into a

co-dependent abusive relationship with their sin.

"Do you want to be healed?"

"Yes, of course, I do. Well, sort of. I am kind of attached to this and that. So change me, but leave me alone in some areas...I'm kind of comfortable."

This kind of question that Jesus asked can remind all of his followers that following Jesus does not come without cost.

Following Jesus will revolutionize your life. It will destroy the walls that years of sin have built, and you will finally be free.

That is change.

Something incredible happens when we are able to voice our urgent needs to the Lord. Physical, emotional, or spiritual.

Can you vocalize your need for Jesus? Can you phrase some sentences, or just utter a few words? Either way is fine with him. Just believe that He alone can rescue and meet your needs.

Vocalizing our need for God is crucial.

Even in order to be saved, we must call out to Him. Jesus knows your need. But the real question is, do you? Do you know your need to be saved and forgiven for your sin?

How are we saved?

For if you confess with your mouth that Jesus is Lord and believe in your heart that God raised him from the dead, you will be saved. Romans 10:9, NLT.

There it is again.

Call out to him.

Vocalize your request.

Communicate your faith that Jesus is the Son of God. He suffered and paid the penalty for your sin. He rose from the dead. He is alive today. He is coming back.

And...He loves you.

"For God so loved the world that he gave his only Son, so that everyone who believes in him will not perish but have eternal life. John 3:16, NLT.

Be urgent. Let nothing else stand in the way of having a right relationship with Jesus.

If you will pardon the metaphorical language for just a moment, I want to tell you how much I see myself in Bartimaeus.

Like Bartimaeus, I was just a blind beggar with patchy knees, weathered and nicked hands, covered in whatever filth I had been crawling through to wait in my spot at the edge of the road. I was bandaged and insecure. I could see with my eyes, but was blind in my heart. Worn out clothes wrapped my shivering body during the cold nights while the wind swirled about my head…a shade tree would cool my sun-burned body in the heat.

Injuries and wounds that would not heal—some wounds caused by my dad—most wounds self-inflicted by choosing to sin instead of choosing to follow Jesus.

I walked bent-over in shame because of the weight pulling me down in my heart. In my heart, I carried the weight of my own sin and the hurt caused by my dad.

I did not know that choking weight was there; I was blind. I did not know why I was so crushed.

The weight was so great that it often became unbearable and I would weep with my face in the dirt, because I could not lift my head.

I was useless. Pathetic. Helpless.

I was a thought not worth thinking. A story not worth repeating. A doomed man. A disgusting, groveling, dirty little beggar.

Then came Jesus!

What he did the night that I was born again is worth telling repeatedly. It is a miracle greater than healing Bartimaeus and restoring his sight.

Jesus healed my heart. He healed my soul. He healed the wounds. He gave me thick robes to keep warm. He lifted my head and removed that weight from my chest.

He placed the weight around his neck, and he stood tall! He lifted me up and wiped away my filth. He looked me square in the eye and told me I was now part of his family. I belonged at the dinner table. His home was my home.

He called me his friend.

I am blessed and proud to follow Jesus in the order of Bartimaeus.

Two blind beggars changed by Christ.

chapter 3

urgent:

a public matter

My little Sofia just turned three years old. I can remember the weeks leading up to Kristy's due date before Sofie was born. Kristy's back ached and hurt so terribly during the night, that she resorted to sleeping on the couch with the hope it would feel better.

She tried to "prop" against me during the night, but I would eventually squirm away. In my sleep, of course.

The last 3 to 4 weeks leading up to Sofia's birth, anytime Kristy said anything to me when I was sleeping; an alarm went off in my mind.

My routine was to jump up and say, "Did your water break?" This happened so often that it became rather annoying to my precious wife.

On November 5, 2007 around 2:00 in the morning—Kristy was sleeping in the living room on the cramped little couch, and I had stretched out on our king size bed snoozing away…Kristy called out…

Joe…

I jumped up.

Did your water break?

I asked her the very same question I had asked all the other times…but this time, she said:

"Yes."

Holy smokes! She said yes! I jumped up, ran into the living room. I crammed the overnight bag into the truck, strapped the car seat into it. I grabbed the zip lock bag of change for the vending machines. I grabbed our camcorder, snacks, took the dog out to use the bathroom, and lined the passenger seat with large black trash bags.

All within the space of about two minutes.

Then, once all my assignments were completed, I walked around in circles in the living room. No reason…just walking… frantically.

I paced from one side of the room to the other…back and forth. Pacing around and around.

Kristy looked at me and said, "What are you doing?"

I have no idea.

Because the time had arrived, there was an urgency to do. Even if that meant pacing the floor, I had to do something. There was an urgency to *do*.

I knew what my responsibilities were…put everything in the car, and drive to the hospital without crashing the car into a tree. Get us there safely. I had already mapped out the shortest distance to the hospital…and made several dry runs in preparation.

Now, suppose instead of jumping out of bed with urgency, that I had rolled over in the bed and ignored her? Suppose I had simply said, "Can't you call your mom? Can't you call our neighbor? I'm kind of tired right now."

Would I have done that? Of course not. Why? Because I had a responsibility to *do*. To move with purpose. I had meaning and significance. I was the only person on the planet who could do what I had to do. It was all mine. What kind of husband and daddy would I have been if I had rolled over and allowed somebody else to do what I was designed to do?

Yet, why do we as Christians treat the church the same way? The majority of Christians leave ministry areas of the church to other people. Let somebody else do it. Anybody else, but not me. We have lost the sense of urgency found in the very first followers of Jesus, found in the Book of Acts. They had an urgency to *do*.

To *do* ministry.

To *do* evangelism.

By using their spiritual gifts, talents and resources.

I find it interesting that the first church began to grow immediately. Those who were first saved and gave their lives to

Jesus Christ and were filled with the Holy Spirit urgently began to share the gospel and do ministry.

When we read the book of Acts, the first several chapters are filled with the church, growing and growing and growing. I am not concerned about that numeric growth they experienced, but I am in the sense that people were being saved. Left and right—wherever you turn in the Book of Acts, people, individuals were being saved. Over and over and over again.

In the temple courts, house-to-house, in the marketplace, in the prisons, everywhere people gathered, the gospel was being shared and lives were being transformed.

Christians were telling others about Jesus and using their spiritual gifts with the purpose of telling others how they could be saved.

Saved from their sins. Saved from hell. Saved from the emptiness that a fallen world brings.

Shortly after I was saved, it seemed odd to me that curriculum existed to teach people how to share the Gospel. I thought, *just tell them how you were saved! Just tell them the difference that Jesus has made in your life. Just tell them that Jesus loves them, died on the cross to pay the penalty of sin, and ask them if they want to be forgiven and saved!*

Why is it that Christians have begun to treat the Great Commission as if it was only a great *suggestion*?

After Jesus was resurrected from the dead, he looked his disciples and followers dead in the eye and said, "Go tell people about me and the things you have heard me teach and do."

Therefore, go and make disciples of all the nations, baptizing them in the name of the Father and the Son and the Holy Spirit. Teach these new disciples to obey all the commands I have given you. And be sure of this: I am with you always, even to the end of the age. Matthew 28:19-20, NLT

For Christians today, I think they read this passage of scripture and somehow walk away with this impression:

"Therefore, it might be a good thing, if you went out to make half-hearted followers of me. Some of them may be baptized, but some won't experience any change at all. Those that are changed should be really, really nice to other people so that, maybe one day, they will be able to earn the right to talk to others about me."

Should we build relationships? Yes. Should we look for common ground? Yes. Is that all we should do? No.

Paul was a born-again Christian just like you. He received forgiveness for his sins, just like you. He experienced the Power of the Spirit of God coming into his life, just like you.

Yet unlike you, he refused to die without telling as many people as possible about Jesus and the forgiveness of sins.

He planted churches, he encouraged churches, he wrote letters to those churches, he visited them, he preached to people about Jesus.

He refused to die wasting his gifts, wasting his transformed life.

Everything Paul did he did because he was focused on telling people about Jesus.

He did not waste his breath; he did not waste his strength. He did not waste his time. If Paul had a Facebook account, he would have used it to share the gospel of Jesus Christ with others.

To the Corinthians he wrote:

So I run straight to the goal with purpose in every step. I am not like a boxer who misses his punches. I discipline my body like an athlete, training it to do what it should. Otherwise, I fear that after preaching to others I myself might be disqualified.
1 Cor. 9:26-27

Paul's goal was to do what Jesus expects his followers to do: Share the good news that Jesus Christ is the Messiah, that he suffered and died on the cross for their sins, and that everyone who believes in Jesus will be forgiven for their sins and have everlasting life.

In fact, telling others about Jesus was Paul's only goal in life. Everything he possessed or owned he considered a loan by

God. Everything he had or experienced was only entrusted or given to him so that he could use it to tell more people about Jesus. Every person he met, he tried to become like them so he could love them and tell them about Jesus (I Corinthians 9:19-23). He summed up the lengthy passage with these words:

Yes, I try to find common ground with everyone so that I might bring them to Christ. I do all this to spread the Good News, and in doing so I enjoy its blessings. I Corinthians 9:22b-23, NLT

We tend to view hard times in life merely as a method God chooses to use to strengthen our faith, and to develop perseverance. But that is not the only way Paul saw the difficult times he faced in life. We think, God must be trying to teach me something, to strengthen my character to become more like Jesus as Peter wrote. Yet, Paul was convinced also that every difficult situation brought him **face to face** with people who needed to hear about Jesus.

Each time he was thrown in jail for preaching the gospel, he viewed it as an opportunity to gain a different audience inside the jail to tell others about Jesus.

Sitting in prison, he wrote these words:

And I want you to know, dear brothers and sisters, that everything that has happened to me here has helped to spread the Good News. For everyone here, including all the soldiers in the palace guard, knows that I am in chains because of Christ. Philippians 1:12, NLT

Can you imagine how your life would change if you began to view the world the way Paul viewed it? The next time you receive a traffic ticket, be convinced that God has given you an opportunity to tell the police officer about Jesus.

If you are in a traffic accident, you have been given an opportunity to communicate to the other driver, your insurance company, the tow truck-driver, the auto mechanic, and the car-body shop about Jesus! If you were injured, now you have been given an opportunity to tell the doctors, medical team, ambulance drivers, the EMT's, and hospital staff about the Great Physician.

We spend so much time trying to find common ground with people around us; yet we miss opportunities staring us in the face.

Your difficult time is your common ground!

Paul was under house arrest and waited at least two years before he was finally able to stand before King Agrippa, so he could argue his case and beg for his freedom. But instead of whining and pleading for his freedom, he used it as an opportunity to share his testimony about being saved and meeting Jesus!

Read Paul's defense to King Agrippa.

"I used to believe that I ought to do everything I could to oppose the followers of Jesus of Nazareth. Authorized by the leading priests, I caused many of the believers in Jerusalem to be sent to prison. And I cast my vote against them when they were con-

demned to death. Many times I had them whipped in the syna-
gogues to try to get them to curse Christ. I was so violently
opposed to them that I even hounded them in distant cities of
foreign lands.

"One day I was on such a mission to Damascus, armed with the
authority and commission of the leading priests. About noon,
Your Majesty, a light from heaven brighter than the sun shone
down on me and my companions.

We all fell down, and I heard a voice saying to me in Aramaic,
'Saul, Saul, why are you persecuting me? It is hard for you to
fight against my will.'

" 'Who are you, sir?' I asked.

"And the Lord replied, 'I am Jesus, the one you are persecuting.
Now stand up! For I have appeared to you to appoint you as my
servant and my witness. You are to tell the world about this
experience and about other times I will appear to you. And I will
protect you from both your own people and the Gentiles. Yes, I
am going to send you to the Gentiles, to open their eyes so they
may turn from darkness to light, and from the power of Satan
to God. Then they will receive forgiveness for their sins and be
given a place among God's people, who are set apart by faith in
me.'

"And so, O King Agrippa, I was not disobedient to that vision
from heaven. I preached first to those in Damascus, then in
Jerusalem and throughout all Judea, and also to the Gentiles,
that all must turn from their sins and turn to God—and prove

they have changed by the good things they do.
Acts 26: 9-20, NLT

King Agrippa, do you believe the prophets? I know you do—"

Agrippa interrupted him. "Do you think you can make me a Christian so quickly?"

Paul replied, "Whether quickly or not, I pray to God that both you and everyone here in this audience might become the same as I am, except for these chains." Acts 26:27-29, NLT

Paul did not whine to King Agrippa and beg for his freedom. He shared his testimony about Jesus; the very reason he had been arrested in the first place!

Arguably, this must have been the most difficult two years Paul had experienced. Living in prisons. Under house arrest. Scoffing and mocking. Yet, he used the difficult time as a tool to talk about Jesus.

Do you treat the difficult times in your life the same way? Do you view them as an opportunity to *do* ministry? To glorify God? Do you know what it is like to shine the Gospel of Jesus Christ, and see it swell like a surging spring into the hearts of those about to accept Christ?

But, you might say, "I'm not Paul."

Big deal.

Neither am I.

I remember immediately after I was saved, I was told to tell others about Jesus. That made perfect sense to me. If somebody had not told me about Jesus—I would be on my way to hell, I never would have experienced true peace and healing.

So I began to tell people about Jesus.

I shared the good news about Jesus with my Nana. She told me I was brainwashed. I told my sister Mary, she cut me off and said, "I know what you are trying to do..." I told my brother Pat. I told the men with whom I worked construction. I told shoppers and workers at the mall. I went door-to-door in Dover, Tennessee, knocking on doors and telling families about Jesus.

Two and a half years after I was saved, I moved to Columbus, Ohio to serve with a church plant. To meet my financial needs, I worked at a child care facility.

I told the cook about Christ, she became born-again. Then she led her family to Christ. I told the kindergarten teacher about Jesus. Then her roommate. They both trusted Jesus to be their Savior. All the while sharing the Gospel with many others who worked there.

I moved back to Clarksville, Tennessee and enrolled at Austin Peay State University. I led a Bible study group in the lobby of my dorm. I led a prayer group in the center of the food court. I told my co-workers in the financial aid office about Jesus. I was a Sunday school teacher and volunteer in the student ministry I was saved in. I led a student named Rocky to Jesus...I led a friend named Mike to Jesus in his dorm room.

Over the summers, I worked at a Christian camp and personally led 30 students to Christ. I used my spiritual gift and I was blessed to lead many others to Christ while in college...

Why do I communicate this? Is it because I want recognition or a pat on the back? Hardly. I want to point this out to you:

I was not a pastor! I was not on a church staff! For much of this time, I had not yet surrendered into ministry!

I was a born-again believer in Jesus Christ. I was convinced then, as I am today, that it was my responsibility to share the good news about Jesus Christ.

A very unhealthy attitude has crept into the church and has taken the wind out of much of what God wants to do. The attitude is that the pastors should be the ones who tell others about Jesus. The pastors should be the ones that do ministry.

It is not the pastor's responsibility to lead your son or daughter, your friend or neighbor, your co-worker or spouse to Jesus.

It is your responsibility. It is my responsibility. The Great Commission was given to us all. We must share in the urgency to communicate the gospel.

There must be an urgency to do ministry with each born-again believer because there are people going to hell unless they hear about Jesus. The amazing thing is that the moment you were saved, you were given a unique and special gift to use as a tool to tell others about Jesus.

"A spiritual gift is given to each of us so we can help each other."
1 Corinthians 12:7, NLT

Paul used his spiritual gifts, people were saved. I have used my spiritual gifts, people have been saved. People around you have used their spiritual gifts, and people have been saved. When gifts are used, they strengthen the church and the church grows through the salvation of those around the church.

Too few Christians are involved in any kind of ministry. They become spectators rather than participants. 'Spectators' do not know the joy of being actively involved in ministry and of seeing God work through them as they use their spiritual gifts.

Areas of ministry are left to a few—which translates to fewer and fewer people trusting in Christ as Savior.

Please do not waste your spiritual gifts. Do not waste your talents, or your connections with others. Use it all to bring people to know Jesus Christ as Savior. Humbly, Paul wrote to the church at Corinth and said:

"Imitate me, just as I also imitate Christ." 1 Cor. 11:1, NLT

Maybe you have realized that up until this moment, you have not been urgent about communicating the gospel through your gifts. You do not know the joy of seeing others saved and using your gifts to sharpen others.

You do not have to settle for that.

chapter 4

urgent:

the King is returning

Thank you for making it this far in our journey together. You have stuck with me through my personal story of how I met Jesus. Together we have examined the life of Bartimaeus and his urgent need for Jesus. We have examined the life of the Apostle Paul and the urgency with which he carried the Gospel.

Richard Ross was preaching his heart out to the crowd of youth pastors and workers about the return of Christ. When he mentioned his Savior, he choked up. When he mentioned the return of Christ, he wiped the tears from his cheeks and kept on preaching.

Cracking voice and all.

There was a reason the first church spoke the truth of Jesus to everybody they met.

They expected the return of Jesus. Soon.

I am convinced that the early Christians were so bold in telling others about Jesus because they lived with the expectation that Christ would return soon. Very soon.

Good or bad, have you ever been expecting somebody's return?

Do you remember sitting outside the principal's office

waiting for one (or both) of your parents to arrive? Do you remember the anticipation you felt as you waited for that white-bearded, red-suited, fat and jolly elf's visit to your home?

Do you remember the inexplicable joy or dread that came with the anticipation?

I need to tell you about a time I was forced to wait for something to happen to me…

In High School—there was one person who was bigger and badder than anybody around. He must have stood about 6'4" and tipped the scales at nearly 300 lbs.

He was a big boy. He was mean as a snake.

In fact, "John" had the reputation for bullying people, beating people up, and staying in ISS (In-School Suspension).

One afternoon at the boat docks after school, a crowd of *booing* and *jeering* teens cheered John on in a fight against a smaller opponent.

John was about to clobber Wheatie. Wheatie was smaller, but wielded a lead pipe like a Samurai sword, swinging it inches from John's head.

This was going to be a good fight. No. This was going to be one of the best. A classic. This was going to be one of the epic battles of all time.

Until.

John pointed his finger at Wheatie and said:

You better put that pole down, or I swear I will kill you. I will rip your head off.

Wheatie looked at the only source of protection, his samurai sword, he held in his hands. The lead pipe that kept John at bay.

And he threw the pipe down.

He threw it down clanking on the paved parking lot. Like a raging bull, John charged in, head down, fist flying, and decimated Wheatie.

John was so bad, that his reputation alone was enough to force Wheatie to rid himself of his only source of protection.

There. That is the picture I want you to have of John as I move into my next story.

He was big. He was bad.

Next to him, I was not.

I was Screech.

I stood about 5'7", and weighed 160 lbs. I was little bitty.

However, I did have a pocketknife.

My Case XX pocketknife. She was a beauty. 2-½" blade. Wooden handle with pearl swirling. She was a nice knife.

And sharp.

She could slice through paper like a hot knife through butter. Many times in class, hiding behind the student who sat in front of me, I pulled her out, and let her slide through the center of loose-leaf paper.

People sitting around me seemed to get a kick out of it. I enjoyed the attention.

Then I made the mistake of showing my knife to John.

Let me see your knife.

I pulled it out to show it off.

He reached out with his big hand and took it from me. He took it from me! In a second, my knife was gone.

I spent the remainder of the year of school plotting the return of my knife. I knew I could not fight him for it. He would kick my tail. There was no way I would tell on him... so I hatched a plan to become his friend and confidant with the hope he would give my knife back to me.

One year later, I sat behind John in our American History class. He turned around and showed me my knife! Blade open and everything. I reached out to grab the knife.

Did I mention the blade was open?

I pulled it away from him, and in doing so, sliced John's thumb from the center-tip of his thumb, to the knuckle.

He didn't even flinch.

He turned back to face the front of class. Motionless for a moment, he sat in silence. He reached down behind him, and tore off a piece of his shirttail. He wrapped it around his thumb to stop the bleeding. Then turned around to look at me.

Without a word, I gave him back the knife.

He turned, rose from his desk. Walked out of the middle of class, and went to the office. The office sent him to the local clinic.

Two hours later, I was called up to the office over the intercom system because John had left the clinic and was returning to the High School to kill me!

The office staff barricaded me into a little room, pushed the desk up to the door and waited for his return.

That was one of the most serious, and dreaded returns I have ever experienced.

The office staff knew he was serious. They took action.

I sense that the first church was just as serious about the return of Jesus Christ.

Sometimes it feels as though the church is in a "lame duck" session. Born-again Christians know that Jesus died and rose from the dead. He defeated death. He forgave sin. We know that Jesus is triumphant.

We are supposed to go, tell and baptize.

Yet we are stuck gawking at the sky. Not necessarily waiting for him to come back.

Just gawking.

Not telling others about Jesus.

Just staring.

Not baptizing.

Just standing around.

Just coasting along.

Just showing up on Sunday to be fed.

Not to feed others.

The church is in neutral.

All we have to do is tell others about Jesus. All we have to do is take the Great Commission seriously.

But we do not.

The church is coasting along. Our attitude seems to be, *if we pick up a few hitchhikers evangelically along the road to heaven that is great.*

Shame on us.

The first church lived under the expectation that Jesus Christ is coming back. Soon.

Jesus came and told his disciples, "I have been given complete authority in heaven and on earth. Therefore, go and make disciples of all the nations, baptizing them in the name of the Father and the Son and the Holy Spirit. Teach these new disciples to obey all the commands I have given you. And be sure of this: I am with you always, even to the end of the age."
Matthew 28:18-20, NLT

It was not long after he said this that he was taken up into the sky while they were watching, and he disappeared into a cloud.

As they were straining their eyes to see him, two white-robed men suddenly stood there among them. They said, "Men of Galilee, why are you standing here staring at the sky? Jesus has been taken away from you into heaven. And someday, just as you saw him go, he will return!" Acts 1:9-15, NLT

Jesus looked his disciples dead in the eye, and told them:

Tell the world about me.

Then he lifted off, floating into the heavens.

That is why those men stood there gawking. That is why they remained as they were. Note that they did not go, tell, and make disciples.

Jesus had told them:

Go – tell – baptize – teach!

Instead, they stood.

Staring.

Now, I understand they were surprised. They were shock-and-awed. But the commands of Jesus could not have been any clearer. They were not made to stand around and stare at the sky. Jesus did not invest three years of his life in ministry on the earth so they would just stand around and stare.

The Lord made it very clear to his followers then, and his followers today that there must be an urgency to tell others about Jesus because time is running out.

The only thing that snapped the disciples out of their gawking stare was the declaration by the two men robed in white:

He will return!

As they were straining their eyes to see him, two white-robed men suddenly stood there among them. They said, "Men of Galilee, why are you standing here staring at the sky? Jesus has been taken away from you into heaven. And someday, just as you saw him go, he will return!" Acts 1:10-11, NLT

Jesus is going to come back.

These words snapped the followers of Jesus out of their trance. He will return. He is going to come back to this earth. Those words are the very same words I believe God wants to use to snap Christians out of their gawking, staring, trance.

We must all go out to tell others about Jesus. We must all seek to live holy lives devoted to him. We must all call out daily for Jesus, as Bartimaeus did when Jesus was passing by.

Peter and the other apostles took the return of Christ seriously and throughout the book of Acts, we see the first church explode with people who are being saved. After the disciples were filled with the Holy Spirit, they went out to tell.

Peter stood up to preach his first sermon and...

Those who believed what Peter said were baptized and added to the church—about three thousand in all. Acts 2:41, NLT

Here we see the number of believers in Jesus—the number of born-again, forgiven for their sins saints, grew from around 500 who were present at the ascension of Jesus, to 3,500.

Then we see that those who were saved began to share fervently and eagerly the good news of Jesus with other people.

...And each day the Lord added to their group those who were being saved. Acts 2:47, NLT

Every day the Lord added to their group those who were being saved....who was leading others to Jesus now? Was it only Peter?

No! It was the people!

Every day, people were being saved, because early Christians understood that time was ticking away...Jesus' return was imminent.

Peter was preaching and leading people to Christ. In turn, the people who were saved led others to Christ.

The preacher and the people. Both of them. Together. Not just the preacher.

After dramatically healing a man crippled from birth, Peter preached another sermon, and the number of born-again believers continued to grow.

But many of the people who heard their message believed it, so that the number of believers totaled about five thousand men, not counting women and children. Acts 4:4, NLT

At this point, it is quite possible that the number of born-again believers had grown to 20,000 factoring in wives and children!

How long did that take? Within a 1-½ to 3-½ year span, an explosion of born-again people began to populate the earth. Through the preaching, through the people.

It began with 12 men, and then grew to 500 followers of Jesus who saw him ascend. Then within a couple of years, at least 20,000 people were born again!

Then, check out how the author of the Book of Acts describes the growth of the church:

But as the believers rapidly multiplied... Acts 6:1a, NLT

Instead of addition, Luke, the author, uses the word multiplied. Now the believers were multiplying!

Friend was telling friend.

Neighbor was telling neighbor.

People were telling strangers.

New believers were leading others to repentance. Left and right people were repenting of their sins and trusting Christ for salvation and forgiveness.

Historians have estimated that by the year 300 AD, the population of born-again believers in Europe alone had grown to 6,500,000.

Within 270 years from the Great Commission! I would give anything for that growth rate among Christianity today.

One Wednesday night in our student ministry, an 11th grade student visiting us for the first time gave his life to Jesus Christ and was born-again. He repented and received forgiveness for his sin.

While blinking tears of joy he said to me:

I am going back to tell all my friends about Jesus. I have so many friends who are just like me that need to know that their sins can be forgiven. This is incredible!

That joy can only be experienced through an encounter with the Living King of Kings. The Messiah. The Savior of the World.

I think Richard Ross nailed it on the head when he wrote about our skewed view of Jesus in his book, *Student Ministry and the Supremacy of Christ.*

Many Christians have a pocket-god. Not the LORD. Not the Great I AM. We have our buddy Jesus.

We keep our little friend Jesus in our shirt pocket and we pull him out when times are tough, and then stick him back.

For many churches, Jesus has lost the mysterious aura surrounding him. We have him figured out completely. And since we know Him, he is reduced to a mascot, to a cheerleader.

I suppose if we could dress up a mascot on Sunday mornings to cheer us on in our worship services, we would. That mascot would be somebody dressed up as Jesus with a cross on his back and a crown of thorns on his head.

Then we would chant across the aisle to the other side of the church:

We love Jesus. Yes we do. We love Jesus. How about you?

The Great Commission is becoming a great embarrassment.

That is why people are not telling others about Jesus—How do we respect in awe and wonder a *mascot* who cheers us on?

Could this be why the church is only growing by 1.38 % instead of by multiplication? We have an incomplete view of Jesus.

We have failed to see the big picture of Christ.

The truth is, Jesus will return to the earth and receive the global glory he did not receive at his birth into our world.

Compare your version of Jesus, to the Apostle John's description of Jesus when he returns:

Then I saw heaven opened, and a white horse was standing there. And the one sitting on the horse was named Faithful and True. For he judges fairly and then goes to war. His eyes were bright like flames of fire, and on his head were many crowns. A name was written on him, and only he knew what it meant. He was clothed with a robe dipped in blood, and his title was the Word of God. The armies of heaven, dressed in pure white linen, followed him on white horses. From his mouth came a sharp sword, and with it he struck down the nations. He ruled them with an iron rod, and he trod the winepress of the fierce wrath of almighty God. Rev. 19:11-15, NLT

Jesus does not sound much like a pocket-Jesus here, does he? His return will be far more spectacular and glorious than we born again Christians could ever possibly imagine.

The sky will split open. Jesus will be riding in on a white horse. Fire from his eyes. The armies of heaven following him. Robe dipped in blood. With his sword, he will strike down nations.

When Jesus resurrected, he resurrected in a perfected body. He was transformed. When he returns to the earth, he will return in his transformed body. After he rose from the dead, people had a hard time recognizing him.

It was Jesus. But, he was different.

On the day that Christ returns, he will return as the Supreme ruler of the Universe.

This Jesus is hard to recognize, because often it is not the Jesus who is preached. We hear about baby Jesus. We hear about crucified Jesus. But we do not hear much about the resurrected Jesus Christ who will return.

The first Church understood that the return of Jesus Christ was right around the corner. They fulfilled the Great Commission with an eye to the sky. With one eye on the people of the world, and another eye watching for the return of Jesus, they fulfilled their calling to the Great Commission.

With an eye to the sky, they lived.

With an eye to the sky, they shared the gospel.

They kept a careful watch for the return of Jesus...they

expected his return any moment. Because they expected his return, they kept telling others about the Good News of Jesus Christ.

Maybe as they thought about his return, they thought about these words:

"However, no one knows the day or the hour when these things will happen, not even the angels in heaven or the Son himself. Only the Father knows.

"When the Son of Man returns, it will be like it was in Noah's day. In those days before the Flood, the people were enjoying banquets and parties and weddings right up to the time Noah entered his boat. People didn't realize what was going to happen until the Flood came and swept them all away. That is the way it will be when the Son of Man comes.

"Two men will be working together in the field; one will be taken, the other left. Two women will be grinding flour at the mill; one will be taken, the other left. So be prepared, because you don't know what day your Lord is coming.

"Know this: A homeowner who knew exactly when a burglar was coming would stay alert and not permit the house to be broken into. You also must be ready all the time. For the Son of Man will come when least expected. Matthew 24:36-44, NLT

Jesus is coming back. While theologians argue about exactly what that will be like, they all agree that our time to share the gospel is running out.

We have a responsibility to learn to share the gospel with Muslims. To learn to share the gospel with those belonging to other faiths, or no faith at all. Do you share the gospel with your neighbors, your employers, your friends, and your family?

We must urgently be sharing the gospel of Jesus Christ with others, because the day of Christ's return is closer than it was 2,000 years ago.

Is your family ready? Your friends? Your neighbors?

Which one of your friends, family, or co-workers should you not tell about Jesus?

Get busy. Be urgent.

The time is near.

To order additional copies of *urgent: igniting a passion for Jesus,* send $11.95 plus $3.00 for shipping and handling to

Free Church Press
P.O. Box 1075
Carrollton, GA 30112

You may also order directly from our website:

www.freechurchpress.com

If your student group is interested in purchasing several copies of *urgent* for small group studies, Free Church Press offers special discounts on bulk orders.

Contact us at freechurchpress.info@gmail.com. Or you may write us at the address above.